STEPHEN F. AUSTIN STATE UNIVERSITY JACKS

FRONT COVER: Lumberjacks and Ladyjacks from each of Stephen F. Austin State University's 15 competitive teams are, from left to right, (sitting) Zach Gardner (baseball) and Monika Covington (softball); (kneeling) Laura Harrison (women's tennis), Tim Knicky (football), and Karla Mason (soccer); Kelli Partridge (golf), Laura Cramer (bowling), Keith Mahipala (men's cross-country), M. C. Bottles (volleyball), Matt Kingsley (basketball), Ebbonye Johnson (women's track), Jordan Ford (women's basketball), John Arthur (men's track), Ricky Wilkenfield (men's golf), and Brittainy Robertson (women's cross-country.) (Photograph by Hardy Meredith.)

COVER BACKGROUND: The background image on the cover shows fans of Stephen F. Austin State University's Southland Conference Championship team watching the Lumberjacks play in the NCAA Division II championship football game against Georgia Southern University in Statesboro, Georgia, on December 16, 1989. The "Axe 'em Jacks" sign depicts a cheer used frequently at Lumberjack and Ladyjack athletic contests. (Photograph by Hardy Meredith.)

BACK COVER: This features coach Jamie Frias and the Ladyjack soccer team, winners of the Southland Conference Championship in 2007—their second. Shown are, from left to right, coach Jamie Frias, Erika Palmacci, Amanda Lackey, Jessica Cotton, Brittany Barker, Kesia Broome, Jenna Turner, Rachel Schwind, Courtney Bauder, Keyli Townsend, Lauren Fricks, Brenna Crockett, Megan Cash, Crystin Pactor, Summer Bradfield, and Erin Lycan. (Photograph by Hardy Meredith.)

STEPHEN F. AUSTIN STATE UNIVERSITY JACKS

Hardy Meredith and Archie P. McDonald

ARCADIA PUBLISHING

To Jeri, Hardy C., Heath Dale, Blake, Jaxon Hardy, and Carley Meredith, and to Judy, Kelly, Tucker, Christopher, and Janet McDonald— Ladyjacks and Lumberjacks all.

ISBN 978-0-7385-7180-5

Published by Arcadia Publishing
Charleston SC, Chicago IL, Portsmouth NH, San Francisco CA

Printed in the United States of America

Library of Congress Control Number: 2009926231

For all general information contact Arcadia Publishing at:
Telephone 843-853-2070
Fax 843-853-0044
E-mail sales@arcadiapublishing.com
For customer service and orders:
Toll-Free 1-888-313-2665

Visit us on the Internet at www.arcadiapublishing.com

CONTENTS

ACKNOWLEDGMENTS

Since Stephen F. Austin State University (SFA) opened its doors in 1923, thousands of athletes and coaches and many more thousands of fans have experienced what Jim McKay called "the thrill of victory and the agony of defeat" on athletic fields and courts and other arenas of competition in the Lone Star, Gulf Star, and Southland Conferences. Each played a role in the Lumberjack/Ladyjack story, and we wish to acknowledge them first. Then, we thank athletic director Robert Hill, associate director Matt Fenley, and assistant director John Branch for seeing the potential in this project and sports information officers James Dixon and Brian Ross and athletic department staff member Crystal Shaw for identifying athletes and providing information about them. Linda Reynolds aided our search in the records of the East Texas Research Center, and Gary Russell, John Levra, Lynn Graves, and Buddy Lowery generously loaned personal pictures for our use. As always, appreciation is especially extended to Portia Gordon for deciphering the publisher's prescriptions and arranging a format that our conscientious and always cheerful editor, Luke Cunningham, would accept.

INTRODUCTION

The Texas Legislature authorized a teacher preparation college in East Texas in 1917 and required that it honor Stephen F. Austin, the Father of Texas, but provided no money to establish the facility for several years. Early in the 1920s, a legislative committee selected Nacogdoches from among several applicant cities as the site for Austin's namesake institution and appointed Dr. A. W. Birdwell, a professor at Southwest State Teachers College, president of the new school. The institution was named Stephen F. Austin State Teachers College for several decades; the word "Teachers" was dropped first, then "University" replaced "College" in 1968. In the 21st century, Stephen F. Austin State University is a full-service institution offering baccalaureate and masters degrees in multiple fields and doctoral degrees in forestry and education.

Among the first staff members Birdwell hired before classes commenced in 1923 was Robert H. "Bob" Shelton, an outstanding athlete at Southwest Texas, who agreed to move to Stephen F. Austin State University and coach everything—literally. Shelton gave up coaching football in 1928 when Gene White took over the program, but he retained head coaching duties in other sports, especially basketball and track and field, much longer, before serving as dean of men until his death in 1964. Since Shelton's tenure, 17 men have coached football, including J. C. Harper, who took over the program in 2007, and 10 coaches have succeeded Shelton in men's basketball, including the coach in 2009, Danny Kaspar.

Over the years other sports were added, including cross-country and indoor and outdoor track, baseball, and golf, and women's athletics changed from an intramural activity to full competition in an even greater number of sports, including basketball, volleyball, cross-country and indoor and outdoor track, soccer, equestrian (now discontinued), bowling, softball, tennis, and golf.

Lumberjacks competed in the Lone Star Conference from 1931 until 1981 and as a member of the National Association of Intercollegiate Athletics (NAIA) until the conference joined National Collegiate Athletic Association (NCAA) Division II. Stephen F. Austin State University joined the Gulf Star Conference in 1983 then moved to the Southland Conference in 1987 as an NCAA Division I member. Ladyjacks participated in competition sanctioned by the Association of Intercollegiate Athletics for Women until 1981, then in the Gulf Star and Southland Conferences. Along the way, both Ladyjacks and Lumberjacks have won multiple conference championships, one national championship, and individual honors as All-American and all-conference athletes, and many have enjoyed successful professional careers in athletics. The greatest number of Ladyjacks and Lumberjacks, however, follow careers in teaching, coaching, business, or other professions. These are the former student-athletes most likely to return for Homecoming activities, to honor former coaches either retired or moved to other assignments, and to remember wearing purple-and-white uniforms and representing their school and teammates as Ladyjacks and Lumberjacks.

This is the story in pictures and words of the players and the coaches and the administrators and trainers and managers and cheerleaders and support staff members—and their fans. We hope both the images and captions help you remember when.

1

BEGINNINGS

From the founding of Stephen F. Austin State University in Nacogdoches, Texas, in 1923 through World War II and the start of the cold war that was its consequence, the college attracted new residents to the city as students, faculty, and staff and always provided the best show in town. That was true for many educational and cultural reasons, but intercollegiate athletic competition contributed every bit as much, and sometimes more, in making Nacogdoches a college town. Games in Aikman Gym or on Birdwell Field and then Memorial Stadium attracted large crowds for games against archrivals from Sam Houston State Teachers College and later Howard Payne and Abilene Christian Universities.

This beginning time is remembered as . . . coach Shelton's era, when one man literally coached every sport . . . the arrival of coaches Gene White, "Red" Willis, M. A. Baumgartner, Bill Pearce, and Ted Jeffries in football and Stan McKewen, Glen Rose, and John O. Stephens in basketball . . . Virginia Broadfoot showing girls how to play basketball . . . June Irwin and Lucille Norton "inventing" the term "Ladyjacks" . . . women playing field hockey and badminton . . . Larry Franks, Van Samford, and Marshall Matterson shooting baskets . . . line coach Ralph Murff, and then nearly all male students, departing for army, navy, and marine corps duty during World War II, leaving 300 or so female students on campus . . . no competitive sports at all between 1942 and 1945 because "there's a war on, don't you know" . . . Dick Wright coming home from the war to lead the Lumberjack football team . . . and getting a new football stadium that doubled as a men's dormitory. These were days of many beginnings, even beginning again after World War II, for the college among the pine trees.

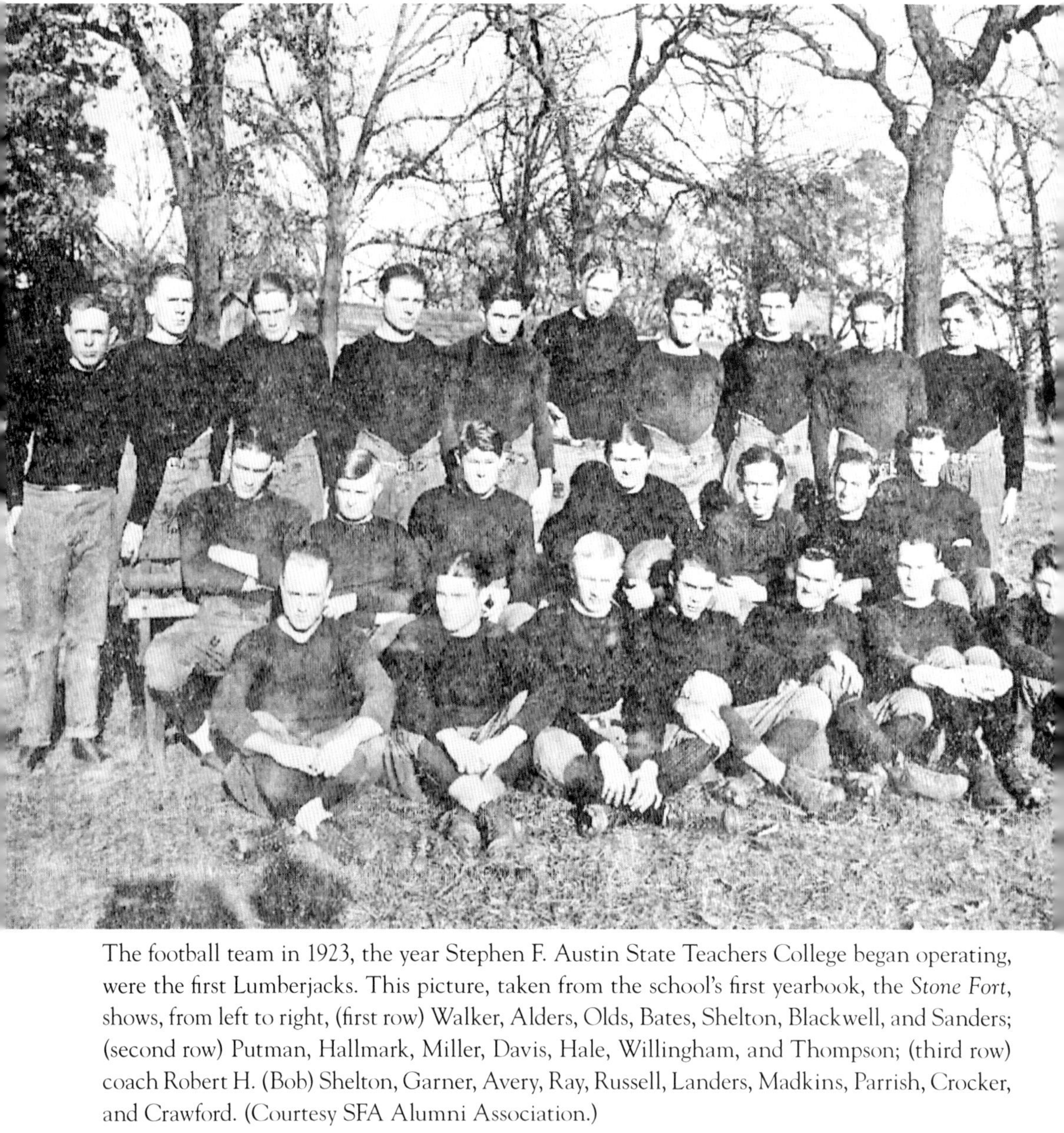

The football team in 1923, the year Stephen F. Austin State Teachers College began operating, were the first Lumberjacks. This picture, taken from the school's first yearbook, the *Stone Fort*, shows, from left to right, (first row) Walker, Alders, Olds, Bates, Shelton, Blackwell, and Sanders; (second row) Putman, Hallmark, Miller, Davis, Hale, Willingham, and Thompson; (third row) coach Robert H. (Bob) Shelton, Garner, Avery, Ray, Russell, Landers, Madkins, Parrish, Crocker, and Crawford. (Courtesy SFA Alumni Association.)

ROBERT H. SHELTON, *Head Coach.*

Just "Coach Bob" Shelton. He's not very big and he doesn't say much, but how he can instill that ol' fighting spirit into the boys. They'll fight for the school and for the coach, too. "Coach" received his training at San Marcos. According to the records he made every team, from "Mumble Peg" to matrimony. Of course, the Lumberjacks didn't capture quite every game the past season; but with Mr. Shelton to show 'em how it's being done, the fall prospects look bad for other Teachers Colleges.

Coach Robert H. (Bob) Shelton, from Dripping Springs, Texas, served as captain of five teams and earned 15 letters in four years of athletic competition at Southwest Texas State Teachers College in San Marcos, Texas, by 1921. Dr. A. W. Birdwell, president-designate of the newly created Stephen F. Austin State Teachers College in Nacogdoches, hired Shelton, a senior, as athletic director for the new school. Coach Shelton, as shown in the *Stone Fort* for 1923, dressed out for practice. The photograph at right shows dean of men Robert Shelton in 1964. (Both courtesy SFA Alumni Association.)

Track and field competition, also coached by Robert Shelton, began at Stephen F. Austin in 1923 and has continued until the present. Members of the squad in 1924 are identified in this photograph in the *Stone Fort* as, from left to right, (first row) Blackwell, Floyd, Willingham, Pitman (with javelin), Hendricks, and Billingsley; (second row) Parker, Bailey, Garner, Redding, Ray, and Baugh. Below, the football team schedule from the 1927 season features "Big Ed" Sharpe, captain and center. (Both courtesy SFA Alumni Association.)

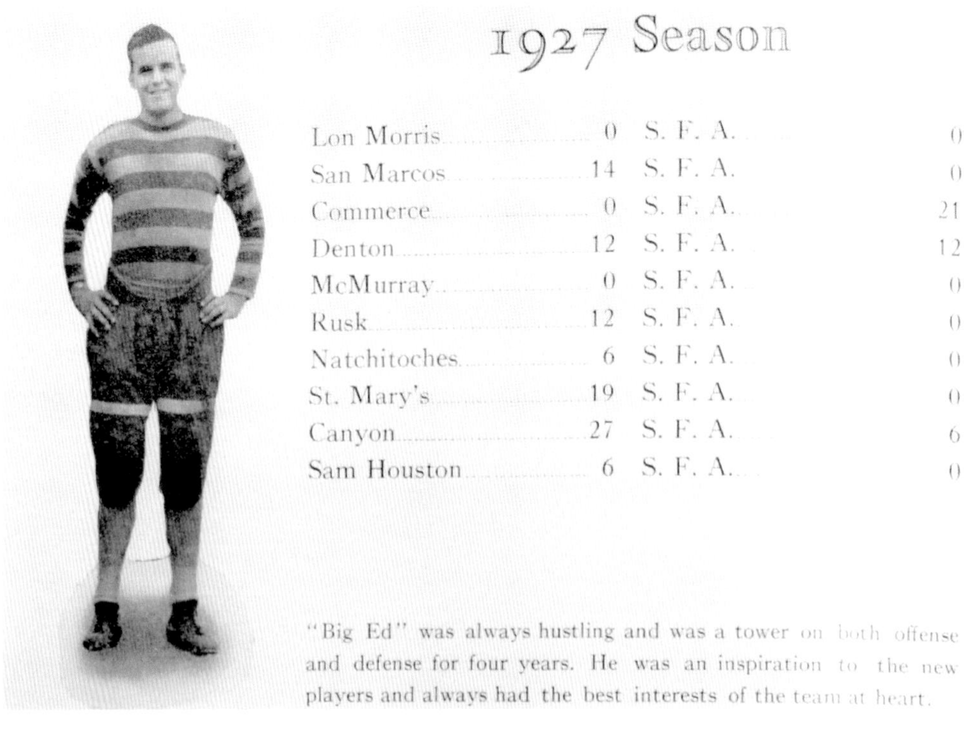

1927 Season

Lon Morris	0	S. F. A.	0
San Marcos	14	S. F. A.	0
Commerce	0	S. F. A.	21
Denton	12	S. F. A.	12
McMurray	0	S. F. A.	0
Rusk	12	S. F. A.	0
Natchitoches	6	S. F. A.	0
St. Mary's	19	S. F. A.	0
Canyon	27	S. F. A.	6
Sam Houston	6	S. F. A.	0

"Big Ed" was always hustling and was a tower on both offense and defense for four years. He was an inspiration to the new players and always had the best interests of the team at heart.

The photograph above depicts action in the Lumberjacks' final game of the season against Sam Houston State Teachers College, played at Birdwell Field on Thanksgiving Day. Below, a Stephen F. Austin pole-vaulter, identified as "Stagner," is shown clearing 11 feet, 6 inches to win first place in a meet between Stephen F. Austin and Sam Houston State. No sand pit appears in the photograph to provide a soft landing for the jumper. (Both *Stone Fort* photographs courtesy SFA Alumni Association.)

The Lumberjack track team, coached by Robert Shelton, was depicted in the *Stone Fort* in 1926. The team included, from left to right, (first row) Golub, Shaw, Claunch, Miller, Rochefort, Johnson, and Stanfield; (second row) George, Pate, Todd, Ainsworth, Koonce, Shoultz, and Henderson. Below, Stephen F. Austin president A. W. Birdwell, standing in a business suit at lower left, poses with track team members and Lumberjack fans at a track meet in Nacogdoches during the 1920s. (Both *Stone Fort* photographs courtesy SFA Alumni Association.)

Ladyjack basketball became a major activity at Stephen F. Austin in the 1970s, but an earlier intramural version of the sport is shown in this *Stone Fort* photograph from the 1920s. Participants are, from left to right, (first row) Pauline Buckner, Loyal Metteaur, and Dalpha Irwin; (second row) Drunetta Nation, Gladys Calloway, Lucille Brashear, Lela Edmonds, coach Virginia Broadfoot, Mable Weaver, Oma Grimes, Anna Belle Lee Burden, and Lorraine Holland; (third row) Nena Flourney, Bertie Rawson, Margaret Lowe, Jewell Davis, Minnie Sealbach, Myrna Holman, Madeline Moore, Reba Crawford, and Charlcey Needham; (fourth row) Angie McNary, Hazel Melvin, Floyd Whittaker, Clara Schenks, Birdie Burkett, Ethel Melvin, Winnie McGaughey, Violet Hanna, Mable Bentley, and Velma Weaver. (Courtesy SFA Alumni Association.)

Virginia Broadfoot (left) was head of physical education for women at Stephen F. Austin in the 1920s. Broadfoot was a graduate of North Texas State Teachers College, located in Denton, Texas. Below is coach Robert Shelton with the men's basketball squad in 1925. Team members included, from left to right, (first row) Haley Bush, Fritz Thompson, Sam Davis, and Grady Bradley; (second row) Shelton, Joe Davis, Ben Tucker, Richard Wier, and James Parker (captain). (Both *Stone Fort* photographs courtesy SFA Alumni Association.)

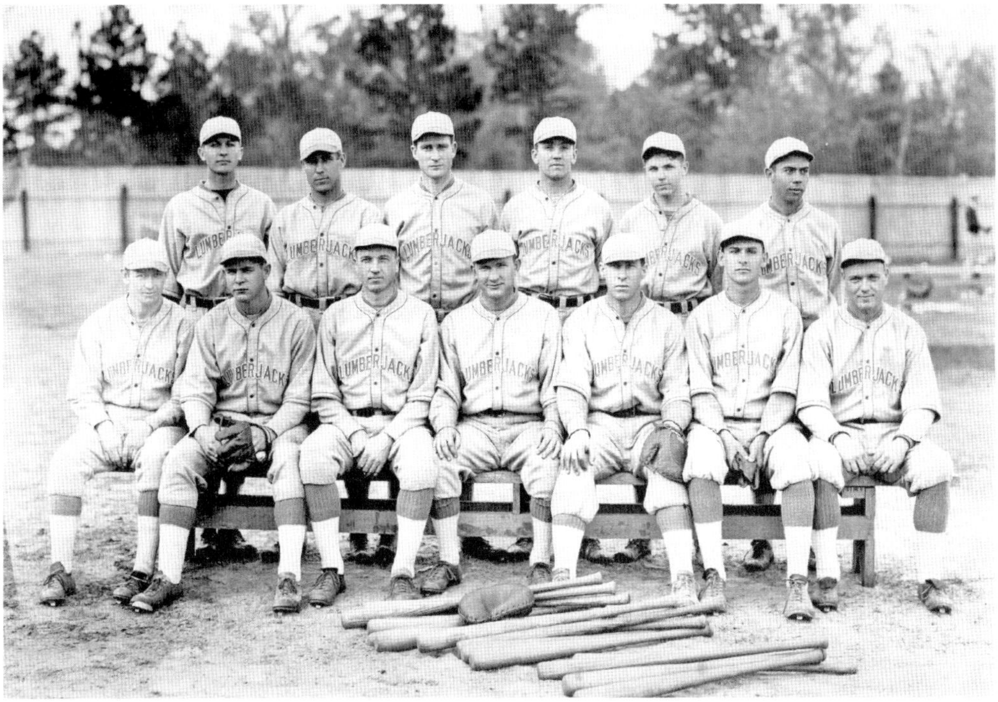

Stephen F. Austin's Lumberjack baseball team in 1926 included, from left to right, (first row) Howard Prince, Joe Davis, Everett Walker, C. N. "Choc" Thompson, Sam Davis, Earl Medford, and D. M. Walker; (second row) Hollis Thomas, Leo White, Lee Conner, Sam Frizzell, Eugene Sanders, and Eura Bates. Below are unidentified members of the pep squad in 1931. They wore white dresses and purple jackets to athletic contests to cheer for Lumberjack teams and also hosted a campus dance in the spring. (Both *Stone Fort* photographs courtesy SFA Alumni Association.)

Above, unidentified women students play field hockey in 1932. The photograph below shows Stephen F. Austin's 1935 football team, cochampions of the Lone Star Conference. Team members included, from left to right, (sitting) Dominy, Little, Bailey, Bush, Mills, Freeze, Hough, McGee, and Barwick; (kneeling) Shanks, Halbert, Sitton, Hurst, Wagstaff, Maberry, West, Lawrence, and Roquemore; (standing) coach Gene White, Gaston, Schillings, Ramsey, Birdwell, Honeycutt, Warren, Porter, Hawkins, McPhail, and line coach Burk. (Both *Stone Fort* photographs courtesy SFA Alumni Association.)

Pictured is the cover of an official program from a football game played against the Sam Houston State Teachers College Bearcats on November 23, 1935, Stephen F. Austin's cochampionship season. The Sam Houston Bearcats remain the Lumberjacks' principal rivals in all athletic competition. (Photograph by Hardy Meredith; courtesy the East Texas Research Center.)

An outstanding Lumberjack basketball player, Lawrence Franks (left) pursued a career in higher education and succeeded Robert Shelton as dean of men at Stephen F. Austin State University in 1964. He later moved to a similar post at the University of Texas, Austin. (*Stone Fort* photograph courtesy SFA Alumni Association.)

A fellow Lumberjack, Van Samford, succeeded Franks as dean of men at Stephen F. Austin. Samford later directed the university's placement office. (*Stone Fort* photograph courtesy SFA Alumni Association.)

Marshall Matterson (right), a major contributor to the success of Stephen F. Austin's basketball teams from 1937 through 1939, later owned and operated the Stephen F. Austin Theatre, a movie theater on North Street one block north of the campus. Below, Emmett Battise, from Livingston, was one of several Alabama-Coushatta Indians who played on Stephen F. Austin athletic teams. Nicknamed "E," Battise played guard. (Both *Stone Fort* photographs courtesy SFA Alumni Association.)

Above is coach Robert Shelton's fifth consecutive Lone Star Conference champion track team in 1936. Members were, from left to right, (first row) Hanigan, Sitton, C. Colwell, Grenshaw, Crawford, and Clayton; (second row) coach Shelton, Ed Hanigan, Tompkins, Jones, S. Colwell, and Irick; (third row) Hawkins, Wagstaff, Honeycutt, Massey, and Ramsey. (*Stone Fort* photograph courtesy SFA Alumni Association.)

Line coach Ralph Murff (left), who worked at Stephen F. Austin State Teachers College from 1937 until he left for military service during World War II, and head coach M. A. (Dutch) Baumgarten, who joined the staff in 1940, are pictured with their sons. Stephen F. Austin State Teachers College did not field teams from 1942 through 1945. (*Stone Fort* photograph courtesy SFA Alumni Association.)

Stephen F. Austin State Teachers College did not field conference athletic teams during World War II, but the student body, mostly women, continued intramural athletics. In 1944, Janelle Tyer (left) and June Irwin won the doubles badminton championship. (*Stone Fort* photograph courtesy SFA Alumni Association.)

Richard Carlyle (Dick) Wright, captain of the Lumberjack football team in 1946, represented the resumption of competitive athletic programs. Wright, a veteran, entered Texas A&M College before the war but decided to return to his hometown to complete his college education. The Dick Wright Award, endowed by the Wright family, annually honors a male athlete who best exemplifies Dick Wright's desire, dedication, and determination as a Lumberjack. (*Stone Fort* photograph courtesy SFA Alumni Association.)

Stephen F. Austin State Teachers College resumed football after World War II with Ted L. Jefferies (left) as athletic director and head coach. Above, Jefferies is shown with, from left to right, assistant coaches Stanford McKewen (also head basketball coach and later registrar of the university), Joe Gallagher, and Harold Fischer, who succeeded Jefferies as head coach in 1956. Below are members of the cheerleading squad in 1950, identified from left to right only as Harriet, Betty, Dana, Nan, and Sue. (Both *Stone Fort* photographs courtesy SFA Alumni Association.)

Shown at right, Elvin (Buddy) Lowery takes a shot in the Shelton Gym during a Lone Star Conference game. Lowery began at Panola College in Carthage, Texas, and then played for the Lumberjacks under coach John O. Stephens from 1957 to 1959. Lowery led the Lumberjacks with 391 points and was named to the all-conference team in 1959. Below, Lowery receives the Todd Memorial Award from Stephen F. Austin State Teachers College president Ralph W. Steen (right) and distinguished alumnus Bob Murphey (left) in 1959. Lowery later played professionally for the Detroit Pistons in the National Basketball League. (Both courtesy Elvin Lowery.)

Aikman Gym, constructed on Stephen F. Austin State Teachers College's campus near the corner of East Austin and Raguet Streets, hosted basketball games and physical education classes from 1924 until the completion of Shelton Gym in 1961. Nacogdoches businessman Frank Aikman donated $12,000 to construct the gym. (*Stone Fort* photograph courtesy SFA Alumni Association.)

Murray Shaw, wearing jersey No. 31, played in Aikman Gym in 1950 and later served as a regent of the university and a successful businessman based in Austin, Texas. The Murray Shaw Reception Room in William R. Johnson Coliseum honors Shaw's service. (*Stone Fort* photograph courtesy SFA Alumni Association.)

Stephen F. Austin State Teachers College Lumberjacks began playing football in Memorial Stadium, located east of Raguet Street on the college campus, in 1946. The stadium was part of a complex that included a park and swimming pool dedicated to the memory of Nacogdoches-area residents who lost their lives during World War II. (*Stone Fort* photograph courtesy SFA Alumni Association.)

The stands on the west side of Memorial Stadium included dormitory rooms, training facilities, and the athletic equipment room. The stadium also hosted commencement exercises and other campus convocations. It was razed in 1972 when Lumberjack Stadium, later Homer Bryce Stadium, was completed. Memorial Stadium's steel bleachers were sold to the Nacogdoches Independent School District and remain in service at Dragon Stadium near Loop 224 in northeast Nacogdoches. (*Stone Fort* photograph courtesy SFA Alumni Association.)

Above, unidentified twirlers in the Lumberjack Marching Band and freshman students line up on the Memorial Stadium field to welcome the Lumberjack football team in 1950. Below, cheerleaders pose before a game. From left to right are (kneeling) Kathy Bratton, John Hamilton and Marilyn Moyers; (standing) George Cannon, Sue Neal, and John McDonald. (Both *Stone Fort* photographs courtesy SFA Alumni Association.)

2

A Middling Time in East Texas

Stephen F. Austin State Teachers College almost ceased operation during World War II. Enrollment dropped below 400 students, mostly females, but resourceful Pres. Paul Boynton, who succeeded President Birdwell in 1942, convinced military authorities to utilize his campus for the Women's Army Corps' first administration school, which brought income to the college and kept its dormitories, classrooms, and equipment in use. After the war, the GI Bill brought the boys back to campus, saving the school, raising the educational level of the region, and increasing the earning power of the students, all at the same time. When Boynton died suddenly in 1957, Dr. Ralph W. Steen became president. Steen promised to work hard to raise the enrollment to 3,000 by 1970; by then, though, over 10,000 were enrolled for classes and Stephen F. Austin had become a full-service university.

Great growth brought many changes to Stephen F. Austin State University between the mid-1950s and 1990. Sprinter Wink Barbin set the track on fire . . . Red Cronkright took over the football program, followed by "Shorty" Hughes, John Levra, Charlie Simmons, and Jim Hess . . . Marshall Brown found the Polnick twins as well as George Johnson, Surry Oliver, Harvey Rayson, Pete Harris, and especially James Silas and made it all the way to the NAIA semifinals in Kansas City in 1972 . . . Sparky Cartwright pioneered competitive golf on campus . . . a new stadium and coliseum replaced Memorial Stadium and Shelton Gym . . . John Levra took his Lumberjacks to the Poultry Bowl, the team's first, and brought a trophy home from Georgia . . . Sue Gunter introduced Ladyjack basketball and took her teams to a national ranking . . . Rosie Walker became an All-America selection . . . Dianne Baker's softball team won Stephen F. Austin State University's only national title . . . and Jim Hess made Lumberjack football successful again.

A middling time necessarily means transition and connection. There are well-begun advances, but the focus inevitably is on the future.

Eugene "Wink" Barbin (left), also nicknamed "The Nederland Flash," led Stephen F. Austin State Teachers College's track team in 1955. Barbin later served as registrar at the university. Below, two standouts of track and field in 1956, Keith Turner (left) and Tracy Pearman, race along the track in Memorial Stadium. The offices of the Stephen F. Austin Alumni Association, located near the Baker Pattillo Student Center, are named in Pearman's honor. (Both *Stone Fort* photographs courtesy SFA Alumni Association.)

Two standout Lumberjacks on Stephen F. Austin State College's football team under the leadership of coach Harold Fischer in the mid-1950s included Jackie Cannon, right, and T. G. (Tom) Evans, below. Jackie Cannon, who served as Stephen F. Austin Alumni Association president, and T. G. Evans remain loyal Lumberjack and Ladyjack fans and attend most home athletic contests. Evans owned T. G. Evans Construction Company, which constructed school buildings, including some on the Stephen F. Austin State University campus, prior to retirement. (Both *Stone Fort* photographs courtesy SFA Alumni Association.)

Robert (Bobby) Sliva played guard on the Lumberjack football team in 1959 and was selected as an All-American on Williamson's Mid-Bracket All-American football team, also know as Little All-American. The selection was based on polls taken in athletic departments from throughout the nation by the Williamson National Football Rating System, a power ranking system chosen by Paul Williamson of New Orleans, Louisiana. The *Dallas Morning News* also placed Sliva on the All-Texas team for 1959, and he was named to the second unit of the All-Lone Star Conference team. (*Stone Fort* photograph courtesy SFA Alumni Association.)

William "Red" Cronkright coached the Lumberjack football team from 1959 through the 1961 season and amassed a record of 6 wins, 25 losses, and 1 tie. Cronkright is shown with his assistants, from left to right, Don Keasler, freshman coach; Ed Lechler, backfield coach; Cronkright; and Mart Crawford, line coach. Crawford remained on the Lumberjack coaching staff for three decades and worked for seven head coaches before he retired. (*Stone Fort* photograph courtesy SFA Alumni Association.)

WELCOME

SFA

EXES

KITTY MORRIS
Homecoming Queen

STEPHEN F. AUSTIN
VS
SAM HOUSTON STATE

HOMECOMING
1968

OFFICIAL
SOUVENIR
PROGRAM
25¢

SFA SCHEDULE

Sept. 14	Angelo State College (H)
Sept. 21	Open
Sept. 28	Northeast Louisiana State (T)
Oct. 5	Delta State (H)
Oct. 12	Texas A&I College (T)
Oct. 19	Sul Ross State College (H)
Oct. 26	Howard Payne College (T)
Nov. 2	Sam Houston – Homecoming (H
Nov. 9	Southwest Texas State (T)
Nov. 16	McMurry College (T)
Nov. 23	East Texas State (H)

DIANNE HUGGINS – MISS TEXAS
Drum Major Lumberjack Band

Shown is the official cover of the program for Stephen F. Austin State University's homecoming game in 1968 against perennial rival Sam Houston State University. Kitty Morris, shown upper left, reigned as homecoming queen, and Dianne Huggins, drum major of the Lumberjack Marching Band and also Miss Texas in 1968, is featured at lower right. The program also lists the Lumberjacks' schedule for the season. (Courtesy East Texas Research Center.)

Joe Richardson joined the Lumberjack athletic staff as an assistant coach under Travis "Shorty" Hughes, head football coach from 1962 to 1978 and track coach and athletic trainer for all Lumberjack teams. (*Stone Fort* photograph courtesy SFA Alumni Association.)

Pictured are head basketball coach Marshall Brown, kneeling, with assistants Ronnie Lusk (left) and Curtis Emmanuel. Brown led the team from 1959 through 1970, establishing a record of 345 wins and only 168 losses. Lusk and Emmanuel played on earlier Lumberjack basketball teams. Lusk, also the team scout, graduated in 1965. (*Stone Fort* photograph courtesy SFA Alumni Association.)

Above, the 1968–1969 Lumberjack basketball team included, from left to right, (seated) James Silas, Terry Brown, Dick Davis, Danny Harris, Matt Scott, and coach Marshall Brown; (standing) Marvin Polnick, Ervin Polnick, Narvis Anderson, George Johnson, Harvey Huffstetler, and Surry Oliver. The Lumberjacks had a season record of 23 wins and 3 losses but were edged out in the Lone Star Conference race by Howard Payne College, so NAIA officials asked the Lumberjacks to represent them in the National Amateur Athletic Union Tournament in Macon, Georgia. George Johnson was named to the National Association of Intercollegiate Athletics All-America team. These Lumberjacks played in Shelton Gym (below), located east of Raguet Street and now part of the Lucille Norton Physical Education Building. (Both *Stone Fort* photographs courtesy SFA Alumni Association.)

Pictured at right are coach Marshall Brown's starting five players in 1969–1970; all five were named to the all-conference team of the Lone Star Conference. From left to right are Ervin Polnick, Harvey Huffstetler, George Johnson, Surry Oliver, and Marvin Polnick. Johnson was named to the first-team NAIA All-America team, Huffstetler and Oliver were named to the second team, and the Polnick twins both received honorable mention designations. Below, coach Brown poses with his star forwards, Ervin (left) and Marvin Polnick, in Shelton Gym. (Both *Stone Fort* photographs courtesy SFA Alumni Association.)

George Johnson played center on four conference championship teams for coach Marshall Brown. He was named to the NAIA All-America team in 1969 and played professionally for the Baltimore Bullets before returning to Stephen F. Austin State University to complete a graduate program in mathematics and begin a career in public education. Johnson still holds the Lumberjack record for rebounds in a four-year career—1,444 in 112 games—and ranks second overall in scoring and rebounding. (Courtesy Department of Athletics.)

Coach Marshall Brown, shown at right in his final season at the Stephen F. Austin Coliseum, led the Lumberjack basketball team from 1959 through 1978. Brown coached the Lumberjacks to 345 victories and 168 losses for a record of .673, the best record of the university's 10 basketball coaches. Below, basketball player Pete Harris receives an award as outstanding player in 1972 from Pres. Ralph W. Steen. (Both courtesy Department of Athletics.)

James Silas (left) and Surry Oliver, teammates on coach Marshall Brown's NAIA finals entry in 1970, when the Lumberjacks finished the season with 29 wins and only one loss, were both first-team All-Americans and were both from Tallulah, Louisiana. Oliver was drafted by Cleveland in the National Basketball Association, while Silas had additional eligibility as a Lumberjack. At left, Silas demonstrates his outstanding vertical jump in a game against the Henderson State Reddies. He later played professionally for the San Antonio Spurs. (Both *Stone Fort* photographs courtesy SFA Alumni Association.)

The William R. Johnson Coliseum was named for Stephen F. Austin State University's fourth president near the end of his administration in 1990. Constructed in 1974 at a cost of $3.4 million, the coliseum is home to Lumberjack and Ladyjack basketball and volleyball, university commencement exercises and concerts, and hosted the NCAA Women's Midwest Regional competition in 1993 and 1996. Major flooding of nearby LaNana Creek in 1976 inundated the coliseum with a water level that measured approximately 12 inches above the baskets, destroying its artificial surface floor. The photograph above shows the muddy water after it had receded approximately four feet. Below, the new hardwood floor is shown. Later renovations resulted in replacing bench seating with chairs, which reduced capacity from 8,000 to 7,200. (Both *Stone Fort* photographs courtesy SFA Alumni Association.)

Ford S. "Sparky" Cartwright lettered in golf for four years, 1965–1969, and was captain of the team from 1966 to 1969. Cartwright's coaches included Carter Franklin, Charlie Simmons, and Mart Crawford, all assistant football coaches. Cartwright's team won the Lone Star Conference championship in 1968 and other tournaments from 1967 through 1969. Cartwright's best tournament score was 68. He received the R. H. "Bob" Shelton Award and was selected for Outstanding Athletes of America in 1969 and for the Jacks of Honor in 1983. He laid the groundwork for futures successes with the golf program. (*Stone Fort* photograph courtesy SFA Alumni Association.)

Lumberjack football standouts for coach Travis "Shorty" Hughes late in the 1960s are shown above. From left to right are (first row) Jerry "Hawk" Clements, Bubba Dosier, Fred Calhoun, Lynn Graves, and Robert Neff; (second row) Bubba Murff, Shub Minter, Don Lorenz, Steve Tackett, and Danny Gilland. Lynn Graves later served as an assistant coach and defensive coordinator with head coach Jim Hess and was head coach of the Lumberjacks from 1989 through 1991. Neff played for the Miami Dolphins in the National Football League. Below, coach John Levra, left, poses with, from left to right, center Curtis LaGrone, linebacker Carl Simmons, defensive back Jimmy Queen, quarterback Gaylan Ramm, and tight end Roland Lytle as they are honored as the team's MVPs at the annual athletic banquet in 1971. (Above courtesy Lynn Graves; below courtesy John Levra.)

At left, Carl Simmons, Lumberjack linebacker for coach John Levra's teams, 1971–1974, receives the Dick Wright Award as outstanding athlete in 1972 from M. Steele Wright, president of Texas Farm Products and brother of Richard Carlyle "Dick" Wright, who was captain of the Lumberjack team in 1946. Below is Mart Crawford, a defensive specialist and assistant coach for three decades under head coaches Travis "Shorty" Hughes, John Levra, Dick Munzinger, Charlie Simmons, Jim Hess, Lynn Graves, and John Pierce. (Both courtesy University News Service.)

John Levra, head coach at Stephen F. Austin State University from 1971 through 1974, led the Lumberjacks to their first postseason bowl game in 1974—the Poultry Bowl in Gainesville, Georgia—where they defeated Gardner-Webb 31-10 and finished the season with a record of 9-3. Above, Levra poses with the 1974 Poultry Bowl MVPs. From left to right are linebacker Sam Hunt, who later played for the New England Patriots; quarterback Larry Mayer; and coach John Levra. Below, Lumberjack backers who accompanied the team and helped bring home the trophy are happy with their team's performance despite the rainy, cold December day. (Above courtesy John Levra; below courtesy University News Service.)

Sue Gunter, the founder of modern women's basketball at Stephen F. Austin State University, coached the Ladyjack basketball team from 1965 through 1980 and also served briefly as women's athletic director. Gunter led the Ladyjacks to five Association for Intercollegiate Athletics for Women national tournaments; coached the U.S. National Team in 1976, 1978, and 1980; served as assistant for the U.S. Olympic team in 1976; and was named head coach for the Olympic team in 1980. Gunter, an inductee of the Women's Basketball and Naismith Halls of Fame, retired with 708 career wins, ranking third nationally in that category. Stephen F. Austin State University celebrated "Sue Gunter Day" on January 26, 2008, the same day the Ladyjacks won their 800th game, an achievement shared by only five other collegiate teams. The Sue Gunter Ladyjack Basketball Office Suite in the William R. Johnson Coliseum honors this Ladyjack legend. (Courtesy Marty McConnell.)

At right, Sue Gunter, founder of the modern Ladyjack basketball program, resigned as women's athletic director at Stephen F. Austin and returned to coaching at Louisiana State University. She brought her Southeastern Conference champion Lady Tigers to William R. Johnson Coliseum to play the Ladyjacks, straining the loyalties of many devoted fans of both Gunter and the Ladyjacks. Below, Gunter's successor, Mary Ann Otwell, calls time-out in a game in 1983. Otwell previously was head coach at Panola College and joined the Ladyjack staff as an assistant coach under Gunter before succeeding her as head coach. (Both courtesy Hardy Meredith.)

Rosie Walker transferred to Stephen F. Austin State University from Panola College and became a Ladyjack legend. She remains the university's single-season scoring leader with 912 points, ranks as the ninth career scorer with 1,561 points, and had a career average of 23.7 points per game. Walker played on the U.S. National Team in the Pan-American Games in 1979 and was named to the U.S. Olympic team in 1980. She was a two-time Kodak All-America selectee and in 2001 was inducted into the Women's College Basketball Hall of Fame. Walker played professionally in the Women's Basketball League for the Nebraska Wranglers. (Courtesy University News Service.)

In 1983, while the cold war remained a fearful reality, evidence that international tensions had begun to thaw came in the form of exhibition athletic contests with teams representing the Soviet Union and the Peoples Republic of China playing teams in the United States. In one such game, coach Mary Ann Otwell's Ladyjacks played the Chinese National Team in William R. Johnson Coliseum. Above, Ladyjack Elaine Wake protects the ball from much taller Chinese defenders. At right, a member of that Ladyjack team, Tammy Mayo, is lifted on the shoulders of teammates in celebration of a victory. Mayo scored 1,844 points in four seasons as a Ladyjack from 1980 to 1984. (Both courtesy Hardy Meredith.)

Stephen F. Austin State University

Nacogdoches, Texas

1976 Lumberjack Football

Charlie Simmons, who had played football at Stephen F. Austin State Teachers College, served as an assistant coach during the tenure of Travis "Shorty" Hughes and was head coach at Kilgore College before returning as head coach of the Lumberjacks in 1976. Simmons led the Lumberjack program through the 1981 season. Shown here on the cover of a game program are, from left to right, (kneeling) Charlie Simmons; (standing) assistant coaches Joe Brittain, Lynn Graves, Mart Crawford, and John Hawkins. Graves later became head coach of the Lumberjacks, and Crawford served as an assistant coach under seven head coaches at Stephen F. Austin State University. (Courtesy East Texas Research Center.)

Dianne Baker coached softball at Stephen F. Austin State University for 15 years and led the Ladyjacks to an NCAA Division II championship in 1986. Baker shows the national championship trophy to fans who had waited for hours for the team bus to arrive from the airport. Baker also served as assistant athletic director from 1982 to 1985 and was inducted into the Ladyjack Hall of Fame in 1987. She later coached at Texas Women's University. In 24 years as head coach, she amassed a record of 764 wins, 473 losses, and 3 ties. (Courtesy Hardy Meredith.)

The Ladyjack softball team won the NCAA Division II national championship in 1986, the only national championship in the university's history. Team members are, from left to right, (kneeling) Kirsten Upcraft, Lisa Abeita, Clare Ashour, Renee Ferguson, Penni Lewis, Lori Eberhardt, Ruth Doxtad, and Paula Tafelski; (standing) coach Dianne Baker, Kathy Walker, Phyllis Aswell, Stella Castro, Kim Clawson, Malisa Waters, Holly Nuber, Michele Savage, Stacy Neiswandor, Mona Cooper, Pam Clay, Renee Smith, and Patricia Wells. (Courtesy J. Lyn Carl.)

The Lumberjacks played football in Memorial Stadium from 1946 until 1973, when Lumberjack Stadium was completed on the eastern edge of Stephen F. Austin State University's campus near University Drive. The stadium's bowl-like construction seats 14,575 patrons, all between the 20-yard lines, and grassy banks increase seating to 25,000 or more. The largest estimated crowd to attend a game was 23,000 fans, who watched the Lumberjacks play the McNeese State Cowboys in 1995. Several high school play-off games have also reached an estimated 20,000 fans. The Lumberjacks defeated Cameron University 17-0 in the first game played in the stadium on September 8, 1973, and have posted a 116-88-2 record there through 2007. The Lumberjacks won four post-season games in the stadium, which was renamed Homer Bryce Stadium in 1986. At left are John Levra (left), the first coach to field teams in Lumberjack Stadium, and Pres. William R. Johnson (right). (Both courtesy University News Service.)

O. A. "Bum" Phillips, who played collegiate football at Stephen F. Austin State University when it was in the Lone Star Conference, coached at Nederland High School, was an assistant coach for the San Diego Chargers, and was head coach of the Houston Oilers and the New Orleans Saints. Two of his Oilers teams played for the American Football Conference championship, losing both times to the Pittsburgh Steelers. Stephen F. Austin State University "retired" Phillips's jersey in 1982. Phillips is shown at right with Dr. Baker Pattillo (left), vice president for student affairs. Below, Phillips, second from left, poses with, from left to right, head coach Jim Hess; Stephen F. Austin State University president Dr. William R. Johnson; Mark Moseley, former Lumberjack and Washington Redskins kicker, whose jersey was also retired; and former Stephen F. Austin State University coach John Levra. (Both courtesy Hardy Meredith.)

Coach Jim Hess, who built Stephen F. Austin State University's strongest team prior to the 1990s, came to Nacogdoches in 1982 from Angelo State University. Hess led the Lumberjacks to a Gulf Star Conference championship in 1985 with a 9-2-0 season, with four wins and one loss in conference play. Hess compiled a 47-30-2 record through the 1988 season and remained for one additional year as athletic director before moving to Las Cruces, New Mexico, to coach at New Mexico State University. Hess later worked as a scout for the Dallas Cowboys. He is seen here posing for a "fashion photograph" that appeared in the *Nacogdoches Daily Sentinel*. (Courtesy Hardy Meredith.)

3

Coming of Age

By 1990, the home of the Lumberjacks and Ladyjacks had become a significant regional university. Stephen F. Austin State University retained its original function as a teacher preparation facility and continued to prepare more professional classroom instructors than any other school in Texas, but it also enjoyed an excellent reputation in many other fields, especially forestry, business, and fine arts. Its science program produced significant numbers of well-qualified pre-medical majors, and liberal arts graduates found success in various professional areas. Dr. Ralph Steen retired in 1976, and Dr. William R. Johnson took over the university for a dozen years. Dr. Dan Angel completed the century as president, then moved to Marshall University and left the leadership to Dr. Tito Guerrero and later to Dr. Baker Pattillo, the first East Texan to serve as president of the region's premier seat of higher education.

Stephen F. Austin State University and its Ladyjack and Lumberjack athletic programs came of age in the 1990s and the first decade of the 21st century. Lynn Graves's Lumberjacks played in a national championship game and despite losing home-field advantage came within one score of bringing home the trophy . . . Mark Moseley, James Silas, and other former Lumberjacks became stars in the National Football League and National Basketball Association . . . Harry Miller came from Kansas to help Lumberjack basketball players win conference championships . . . Sue Gunter moved to Louisiana State University, but a few years later, Gary Blair had the Ladyjacks on top again . . . Sandy Miller and Loree McCary kept their players healthy . . . John Pearce's Posse raised the excitement level higher in Homer Bryce Stadium, and always with class . . . Steve McCarty and Robert Hill oversaw the development of an excellent staff of coaches and support personnel . . . Debbie Humphries's volleyball team dominated the Southland Conference . . . Phil Olson's track and field teams dominated the conference . . . and Jamie Frias's soccer team won two championships.

The modern world is much different from the university's beginning in 1923, including expansion from a hundred or so students to 12,000, a faculty counting less that two dozen to nearly 500, and a campus of two buildings to modern dormitories, parking garages, stadia, recreational facilities, student centers, and more. But "Ax'em Jacks" is a constant that spans more than eight decades. Go, Ladies! Go, Jacks! Purple Power!

Mark Moseley, who played at Livingston High School, is one of the Lumberjacks who made a successful transition to the National Football League. Moseley, who played for Stephen F. Austin State University from 1967 though 1969, was drafted by the Philadelphia Eagles and played the 1970 season there. Moseley moved to the Houston Oilers and Washington Redskins before finishing his career with the Cleveland Browns, but he enjoyed his greatest success during his tenure as a Redskin from 1974 through 1986. Moseley leads that team in scoring with 1,207 points. In his professional career, Moseley, the last straight-on placekicker in the National Football League, made 300 of 457 field-goal attempts, or 65 percent, and scored 482 extra points in 512 attempts, or 92 percent. He scored a total of 1,382 points. Moseley was named the league's Most Valuable Player in 1982. (Courtesy Washington Redskins.)

Mark Moseley (above) returned to Stephen F. Austin State University in 1983 when Dr. Baker Pattillo, vice president for student affairs, announced the retirement of Moseley's No. 10 Lumberjack jersey. The next year, Dr. Pattillo (right) also announced the retirement of No. 41, the jersey number worn by standout Lumberjack basketball player and San Antonio Spur James Silas. Both Moseley and Silas were extraordinary collegiate players who represented the university well in their respective professional careers. (Both photographs by Hardy Meredith.)

Coach Harry Miller moved from Kansas to succeed Marshall Brown as head basketball coach of the Lumberjacks in 1978 and remained through the 1988 season before retiring. Miller's teams won 170 games and lost only 112 games for a percentage of .603. He coached teams in the Lone Star Conference, Gulf Star Conference, and the Southland Conference. Coach Miller holds the distinction of coaching Stephen F. Austin teams in three divisions of post-season play—the NAIA national tournament in 1982, the NCAA Division II tournament in 1983, and the National Invitational Tournament (NIT) in 1987. Danny Kaspar, one of Miller's assistant coaches, later became head coach of the Lumberjacks. Miller retired in Nacogdoches in 1988. (Courtesy University News Service.)

Above, coach Harry Miller is interviewed by Robert Warren Hill, co-owner of the radio station KEEE/KJCS and the "Voice of the Lumberjacks" who provided play-by-play coverage of Lumberjack football and basketball games for 30 seasons. After selling his interest in the radio station in 1987, Hill, a former high school quarterback and lifelong sports enthusiast, became director of sports information at Stephen F. Austin State University. Hill moved to assistant athletic director for business affairs in 1990 and associate director in 1998. He became the university director of athletics in 2005. Below, basketball fans who specialized in inhospitality for visiting teams playing in William R. Johnson Coliseum show disdain and pride for floor action and their belief that their team was No. 1. (Both courtesy Hardy Meredith.)

The overhead scoreboard in William R. Johnson Coliseum welcomes coaches, players, and fans to the NAIA District IV playoffs held in Nacogdoches in 1982. The Lumberjacks eventually lost the game to the team from Saint Mary's, 51-44. At right, Dan Ostrander, who played for coach Harry Miller in 1982, takes a shot in a game against Abilene Christian College, a Lone Star Conference rival. The Lumberjacks won the game, 80-62. (Both photographs by Hardy Meredith.)

Dr. Harold Hill, faculty representative and chairman of the Intercollegiate Athletic Committee, joined the faculty of Stephen F. Austin State University in 1966. Pres. Ralph W. Steen appointed Hill to the athletic committee the following year, and in 1969, Dr. William R. Johnson asked him to chair it. Hill's tenure as chairman of the committee lasted until 1989, the longest in school history. As faculty representative to the Lone Star Conference, Hill kept all records concerning scholastic eligibility and any conference records involving Stephen F. Austin State University. Hill participated in the interview process for the hiring of all coaches between 1967 and 1989. He was a professor of secondary education and educational administration. (Courtesy University News Service.)

Track and field competition has remained an important part of Stephen F. Austin State University's athletic department since coach Robert H. "Bob" Shelton assembled the first team in 1923. Through the years, events developed for both women and men athletes, and competitions were divided into indoor and outdoor seasons as well as cross-country. Above, from left to right, Mike Keck, Jimmy Evans, Mike Braly, Robert Coronado, Dion Lampe, and Jamie Lunsford were members of the cross-country team in 1988. Below, Lumberjack football players honored in 1985 included, from left to right, Rick Wilson, kicker with 51 career field goals; James Noble with 3,035 career receiving yards; Floyd Dixon with 2,819 receiving yards; and Melvin White, four-year letterman, 1982–1985. (Both courtesy University News Service.)

Sue Gunter (center), the founder of modern Ladyjack basketball in 1972, moved to Baton Rouge in 1980 to coach the Louisiana State University Lady Tigers. When Gunter brought her LSU team to Nacogdoches to play against Gary Blair and the Ladyjacks, she was greeted by close friends, seen here. From left to right are Virginia Matthews, June Irwin, Gunter, Alvera Griffin, and Carolyn Mitchell. (Courtesy University News Service.)

Ladyjack Katrina Price gets ready to shoot the basketball. Price was a three-time All–Southland Conference selection and two-time conference Player of the Year. She is the Ladyjacks' all-time leading scorer with 2,278 points. (Photograph by Hardy Meredith.)

Coach Gary Blair succeeded Don Wilhelm as coach of women's basketball at Stephen F. Austin State University in 1985, coached the Ladyjacks until 1993, and left his mark on the program forever. Blair was an excellent basketball coach, but he also proved to be an exceptional promoter of his team and women's basketball in general. His 210 victories produced a winning percentage of .830, the best in Ladyjack history. Blair's Ladyjacks enjoyed seven 20-win seasons, and Blair was named Southland Conference Coach of the Year five times. Blair left Stephen F. Austin State University to coach women's basketball at the University of Arkansas and later moved to Texas A&M University. (Photograph by Hardy Meredith.)

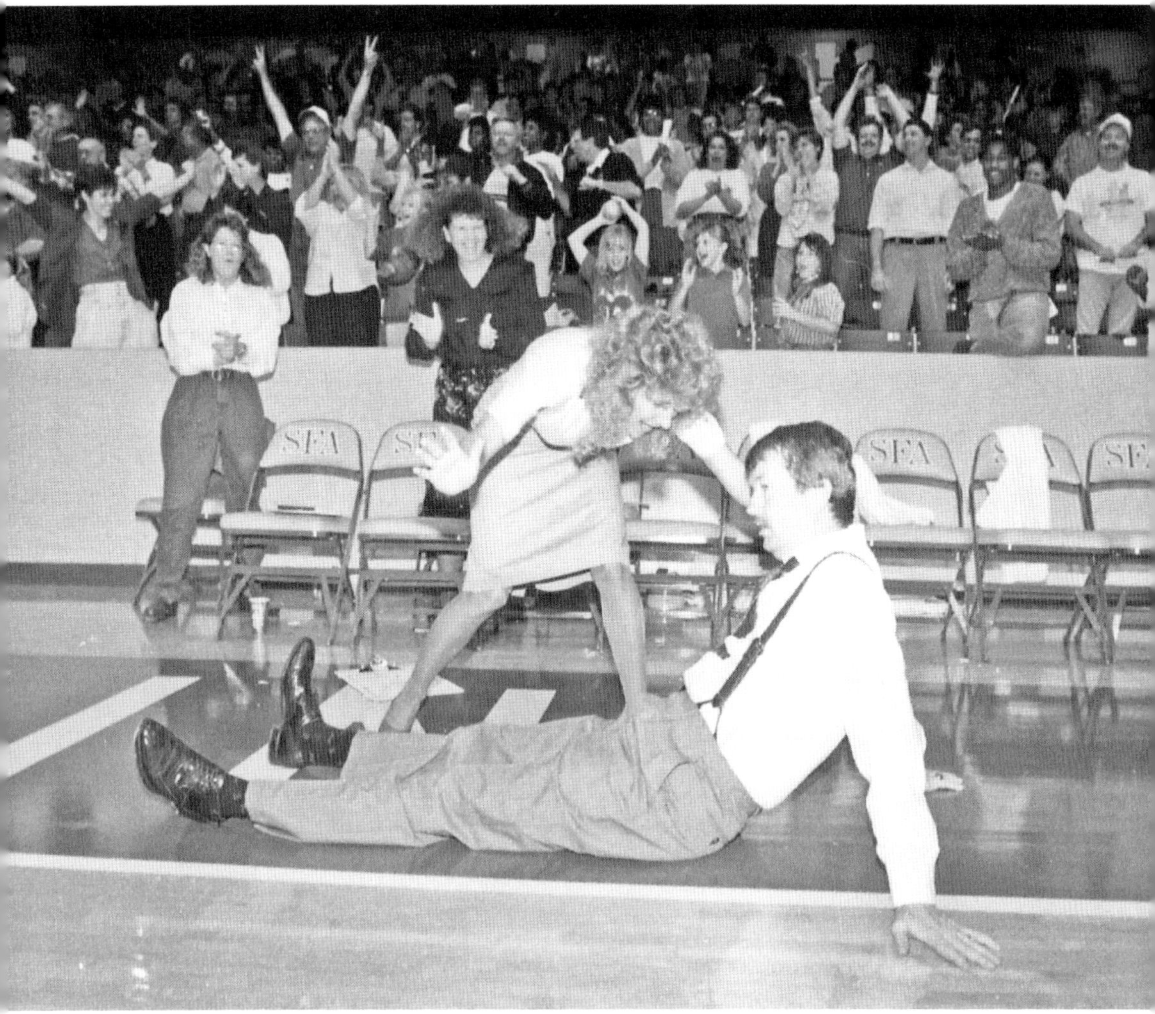

Gary Blair's teams always provided plenty of excitement for Ladyjack fans, as the picture above illustrates, and sometimes for Blair himself. Blair fell to the floor in exhaustion after his Ladyjacks defeated the Louisiana Tech Techsters in 1990, 77-74, with a shot at the buzzer. Assistant coach Julie Thomas both congratulates and shows concern for Blair's exhausted condition as pandemonium continued among over 6,000 Ladyjack fans packed into William R. Johnson Coliseum. Assistant coaches Windy Hopson (standing left) and Lisa Farrell (standing center) look on. (Photograph by Hardy Meredith.)

At left, Antoinette Norris prepares to take the shot while teammate No. 34 (unidentified) looks on in a game in 1988 that gave her temporary custody of Stephen F. Austin State University's Ladyjack scoring record. Below, coach Gary Blair presents Norris with a game ball commemorating her achievement. Norris remains the Ladyjacks' second all-time scorer with 2,062 career points and has the school's seventh highest scoring average at 17.2 points per game. She is the school's second all-time rebounder with 1,360 and third in field-goal percentage with .570. Norris was named Southland Conference Player of the Year in 1988 and played professionally in Spain. (Both photographs by Hardy Meredith.)

"The Express Rolls on" summarizes the Gary Blair era of Ladyjack basketball. The cover of the media guide for the Ladyjacks' 1988–1989 season features, from left to right, Connie Cole, Dayna Reed, Evelyn Butler, Stacy Miller, Ylondra Douglass, and Blair. That season, the Ladyjacks were 30-4-0 with 13 conference game wins and only one conference loss to Northwestern State University. The Ladyjacks of 1988–1989 won their second straight Southland Conference title and finished the season ranked 11th in the nation. (Photograph by Greg Patterson.)

Jim Hess retired as head football coach in 1988, and a longtime assistant in the program, Lynn Graves, who had played at Stephen F. Austin State College and worked his way up through the assistant ranks to defensive coordinator, finally got a chance to become head coach—and he made the most of it. The Lumberjacks won the Southland Conference title that year. The picture above shows Graves leaving the field after the Lumberjacks clinched the conference title. Below, Dr. William R. Johnson, left center, congratulates Graves while Dr. Baker Pattillo, center, beams his approval. At left is Lumberjack supporter and future regent Ron Adkison of Henderson. (Both photographs by Hardy Meredith.)

Quarterback Todd Hamel led the Lumberjacks to the Southland Conference Championship in 1989, the first outright conference championship in football in school history, through NCAA Division I-AA playoff victories over Grambling State University, Southwest Missouri State University, and Furman University. Hamel and the Lumberjacks finally lost in the national championship game against Georgia Southern University in Georgia Southern's home stadium in Statesboro, Georgia, 37-34. Here Hamel celebrates the completion of a touchdown pass in the playoff game against Grambling, and with Hamel are Lumberjacks Jeff Moore, No. 63, and Larry Centers, No. 37. (Photograph by Hardy Meredith.)

In that 1989 championship season, Stephen F. Austin State University faced Grambling State University and its legendary coach, Eddie Robinson, in the first playoff game in Homer Bryce Stadium. This photograph shows Lumberjack coach Lynn Graves, left, greeting Robinson before the game. A fan who witnessed the offensive shootout said, "It was obvious that the last team with the ball would win." The Lumberjacks won 59-56. Below, running back Larry Centers works his magic in a game against the Sam Houston Bearcats during that championship season. (Both photographs by Hardy Meredith.)

Gary Russell, a graduate of Nacogdoches High School and a Lumberjack, celebrates victory in a playoff game in 1989, one of three matchups the Lumberjacks played on their way to the national championships in Statesboro, Georgia. Russell remained in Nacogdoches, his hometown, after graduation and became a successful financial advisor. He remains a devoted fan of all Lumberjack athletics, especially football. (Courtesy Gary Russell.)

Michael Pearce (No. 17) played wide receiver on several Lumberjack teams (1992, 1993, 1995, and 1996) and was coached by his father, John Pearce, who had four teams with national rankings. Michael, called "Raven" in the huddle when passes would be thrown to him, caught 157 passes for 1,777 yards, had nine touchdowns, and ranks second on the SFA all-time list in career receiving yards. Shown below is the NCAA Midwest Regional tournament in women's basketball held at the William R. Johnson Coliseum. (Left courtesy Bill Sloan; below photograph by Hardy Meredith.)

Coach Gary Blair's Ladyjacks won the Southland Conference in 1992 with 28 victories and only 3 defeats and had a conference record of 17-1. The Ladyjacks finished the regular season ranked fourth in national polls and advanced to the second round in NCAA playoffs. Team members are, from left to right, Lori Davis, unidentified, Deneen Parker, Leigh Ann Hicks, Stacy Brown Hairgrove, Kim Spencer, Lynn Corn, Melissa Peay, Stacye Jackson, and Latosha Lewis. (Photograph by Hardy Meredith.)

Sandy Miller is the head athletic trainer who oversees a comprehensive program that cares for current athletes and prepares students for careers as athletic trainers. A native of Kansas, Miller spent five years as athletic trainer for Northwest Missouri State University before moving to Stephen F. Austin State University in 1981. Miller is a member of the board of directors of the National Athletic Trainers' Association and has worked on Olympic, Goodwill Games, and World Championship games teams. He has been honored as Most Distinguished Athletic Trainer, one of 12 in the United States, by the National Athletic Trainers' Association. (Courtesy University News Service.)

One of the most bizarre games played in the newly named Homer Bryce Stadium is remembered as the 1986 "Fog Bowl." The Lumberjacks played the Northwestern State University Demons in a Gulf Star Conference game and a thick fog rolled across the stadium during the first half of the game. Fans on opposite sides of the stadium could not see each other or any action on the field past midfield. Here quarterback Todd Whitton tosses the ball to avoid an unidentified Northwestern player. (Photograph by Hardy Meredith.)

Chuck Rawlinson, Stephen F. Austin's barefoot kicker, holds the school's record for most points, most extra points made and attempted, most field goals made and attempted, and longest field goal—58 yards—against Sam Houston State University in 1991. (Photograph by Hardy Meredith.)

John Pearce (above, second from left) was appointed head football coach of the Lumberjacks after the 1991 season and remained at Stephen F. Austin State University through the 1998 season. Pearce's teams won 46 games, lost 32, and had 2 ties. His teams were ranked nationally in NCAA I-AA competition five times. With Pearce are, from left to right, athletic director Steve McCarty, Stephen F. Austin State University president Don Bowen, and vice president for student affairs Baker Pattillo. Below, in 1993, Stephen F. Austin State University's new president, Dan Angel, second from left, is joined by, from left to right, head women's basketball coach Gary Blair, head football coach John Pearce, and head basketball coach Ned Fowler, each proclaiming his team "No 1." (Both courtesy University News Service.)

Hiram Harrison jumps for a shot in a game against Sam Houston State University in 1982. The game was played in Huntsville at the Lone Star Conference tournament. Harry Miller, who became Lumberjack head coach of men's basketball at Stephen F. Austin State University in 1978, led his team to the conference championship in the 1981–1982 season. In 2009, Harrison coached the Center High School Roughriders, located in Center, Texas. (Photograph by Hardy Meredith.)

Trinia Tillis (left) goes up for jump shot in a game played against Louisiana State University in Nacogdoches in the William R. Johnson Coliseum. Tillis was a three-time All –Southland Conference player and, in 1994, was named Southland Conference Player of the Year. She is the Ladyjacks' eighth all-time scorer with 1,584 career points, ninth in school history in rebounds with 817, and fourth in blocks with 104. Tillis's 47 blocks during 1991–1992 ties her for sixth in team history. Tillis played professionally in Spain before returning to Texas to become head coach at Tyler Junior College in Tyler, Texas. Below, Scott Dimack scores on a layup in a game played in Nacogdoches. (Both photographs by Hardy Meredith.)

Jim McKay of the *Wide World of Sports* program on ABC-TV made the phrase "The thrill of victory, the agony of defeat" as famous as sports themselves; this photograph of Ladyjack basketball player Trinia Tillis personifies the agony. Tillis leans against the wall of the tunnel in the William R. Johnson Coliseum that connects dressing areas and the playing court following the Ladyjacks' loss to Vanderbilt University in the Midwest Regional tournament in 1993. The Ladyjacks led the game in the second half until the shot clocks malfunctioned. After a 15-minute delay, a refreshed Vanderbilt team came back to win the game 59-58. (Photograph by Hardy Meredith.)

Harry Miller served as men's basketball coach at Stephen F. Austin State University from 1978 through 1988 and posted a winning percentage of .603 in 282 games, winning 170 games. Miller's successor, Mike Martin, coached for two seasons, winning 12 games and losing 39. In 1990, Ned Fowler became the Lumberjacks head coach and in nine seasons improved the Ladyjacks' winning percentage to .473 with 78 victories and 87 losses. Here, Fowler, left, follows floor action intently while, from left to right, assistant coach Trey Medlock, an unidentified assistant coach, and Lumberjack Deric Moten look on. (Courtesy University News Service.)

John Pearce, an assistant coach of the Texas A&M Aggies, became head coach of the Lumberjack football team in 1991 and remained in Nacogdoches seven seasons before becoming an assistant coach at UCLA. Pierce wears a cap proclaiming "Pearce's Posse," a nickname for the Lumberjack football team during his tenure, in a post-game interview. (Photograph by Bill Sloan.)

Pearce's staff, featured here, is as follows, from left to right: (first row) Sandy Miller, Kevin Lykins, David Hughes, Pearce, Eddie Brister, Denzil Cox, and Chip Davis; (second row) Chris Roberson, Robert McFarland, David Gibbs, Craig Bailey, Gene Chizik, Rich Rhoades, and Curtis Luper. Brister, McFarland, Chizik, and Rhoades all later became head coaches, McFarland at Stephen F. Austin State University. (Photograph by Bill Sloan.)

Firing "Old Cotton" is a longtime tradition in Homer Bryce Stadium when the Lumberjacks score a touchdown, extra point, or field goal. The artillerists are members of the ROTC program at Stephen F. Austin State University. The cannon is named for Lt. Gen. O. R. "Cotton" Whiddon, Ret., a Stephen F. Austin State University graduate. Below is Homer Bryce of Henderson, former athlete and regent of Stephen F. Austin State University, for whom Lumberjack Stadium was renamed in 1986. The press box, located atop the west stands, underwent extensive renovation in 2003, including adding a third level and luxury suites and seating for Touchdown Club members on the first level. (Both photographs by Hardy Meredith.)

Pictured at right are Steve McCarty, left, and Homer Bryce, right, on "Homer's" field at Homer Bryce Stadium. McCarty, a student-athlete at Stephen F. Austin State University, coached in several high school venues, including Orangefield and the South Park Greenies in Beaumont before accepting the head coaching position at Nacogdoches High School in 1984. He took the NHS Dragons to their first district championship in over a decade and then accepted a position as assistant athletic director at Stephen F. Austin State University when Jim Hess was director and head coach of the Lumberjacks. McCarty became athletic director in 1990, when Hess moved to New Mexico State University. Bryce supported all athletic programs at Stephen F. Austin. Below, the photograph catches McCarty leading his traditional cheer, "Two bits." (Both photographs by Hardy Meredith)

The game is football, and here are two Lumberjacks with talented feet that helped their team win games. Left, kicker Christian Fontana, a former Nacogdoches High School Golden Dragon, scores three points on a field goal for his team. The holder is backup quarterback Clint Bounds. (Photograph by Hardy Meredith.)

Punter Chad Stanley kicks the ball deep to give the Lumberjack defense an edge in stopping the opponent's offense. Stanley holds Lumberjack records for highest single season average of 46.6 yards, career average of 43.3 yards, and longest punt at 79 yards. Stanley played professionally for the San Francisco 49ers, Arizona Cardinals, Houston Texans, and Indianapolis Colts. (Photograph by Hardy Meredith.)

Two of the outstanding Lumberjack football players included Cally Belcher, at right, and Jeremiah Trotter, below. Belcher was a two-time All–Southland Conference team member who started and played in 33 games as a Lumberjack before his untimely death. He recorded 191 tackles, including 140 solo stops, with 5 sacks and 18 pass deflections. Trotter played linebacker for three seasons under coach John Pearce before moving on to a professional career with the Philadelphia Eagles, Washington Redskins, and Tampa Bay Buccaneers. (Both photographs by Hardy Meredith and University News Service.)

Two memorable Lumberjack football players were Larry Centers, left, and Eric Lokey, No. 96 below. Centers, an offensive standout on teams coached by Jim Hess and Lynn Graves, technically played running back but caught as many passes coming out of the backfield as most receivers. Centers spent more than a decade with the Arizona Cardinals in the National Football League, then moved to the Washington Redskins and Buffalo Bills before finishing his career as a New England Patriot. Lokey was a linebacker for the Lumberjacks and returned to coach that position in 2008. (Left, photograph by Hardy Meredith; below, photograph by Greg Patterson.)

Bill Hill guided Lumberjack golfers to Southland Conference championships in 1991 and 1999 and was named the conference's Coach of the Year in 1991 and 1996. His teams included 17 all-conference athletes and two Players of the Year. In 1996, Hill's golf team participated in the NCAA Regional Championships, the Lumberjacks' only appearance in the NCAA tournament. (Photograph by Hardy Meredith.)

Royce Chadwick coached the Ladyjack basketball team from 1994 to 2001. His teams won 173 games and lost 44. Chadwick was named Coach of the Year in the Southland Conference in 1997. Under his leadership, the Ladyjacks won five regular season-championships and six tournament championships. They made seven NCAA tournament appearances. (Photograph by Hardy Meredith.)

Mel Montgomery, who directed the Lumberjack Marching Band for two decades, leads his band in the "Star-Spangled Banner," which is played before all athletic contests at Stephen F. Austin State University. Unidentified assistant directors and a drum major look on. Lumberjack band members are among the most ardent Lumberjack fans and usually make one or two road trips with the football team during the season. A smaller pep band, the "Roarin' Buzzsaws," also plays at all Ladyjack and Lumberjack home basketball games. The Lumberjack Marching Band also hosts several marching contests for area high school bands. (Courtesy Marty McConnell.)

Stephen F. Austin State University took part in baseball competition in the Southland Conference from 1988 through the 1998 season and then discontinued competition for nearly a decade. In 2005, Donnie Watson, a former assistant coach at Texas Christian University, came to Stephen F. Austin State University to reorganize the team and coached for three seasons. (Photograph by Hardy Meredith.)

Uniforms await the arrival of the Lumberjack baseball team in the team's dugout. The Lumberjacks play baseball off campus in Nacogdoches on the Jaycees field in the Pete Smith Baseball Complex. Their facilities received a complete renovation in 2008. (Photograph by Hardy Meredith.)

Lumberjack baseball team members Steven Hill, Jared Pitts, Jake Leonhardt, and David Miller were drafted by major league teams after the 2007 season, and Hill, shown above, was also an All-America selection by the Louisville Slugger and American Baseball Coaches Association. He is the only Lumberjack baseball player ever selected for All-America honors and was named Hitter of the Year for the Southland Conference in 2007. Hill led the Southland Conference with 24 home runs, 73 RBIs, 71 runs scored, and a slugging percentage of .818. The St. Louis Cardinals drafted Hill in the 13th round. (Photograph by Hardy Meredith.)

After an interruption that lasted nearly a decade, Stephen F. Austin State University resumed baseball competition in the Southland Conference in 2006. The photograph above shows coach Donnie Watson's Lumberjack team taking the field in their home opener. At right, Johnny Cardenas became a Lumberjack assistant coach in 2006 as recruiting coordinator and coach of catchers. Cardenas played baseball professionally for six years with the Oklahoma City 89ers and the Duluth Superior Dukes in the Chicago White Sox and Seattle Mariners' organizations before turning to coaching. Cardenas became head coach of the Lumberjack baseball team in 2008. (Both photographs by Hardy Meredith.)

Dr. Tito Guerrero became the seventh president of Stephen F. Austin State University after serving as president of the University of Southern Colorado in Pueblo, Colorado. Guerrero served as a manager of the Aggie football team while enrolled as an undergraduate at Texas A&M University and remained a strong sports enthusiast. Guerrero is shown here making a grand entrance with an unidentified motorcycle driver at the annual "Meet the Lumberjacks" program, held in 2002 at Hotel Fredonia. Guerrero flies the SFA flag, demonstrating his support for his new affiliation. (Photograph by Hardy Meredith.)

George Van Linder became the sixth head coach of the Ladyjack soccer team in February 2008 after coaching at Baylor University for the previous five seasons, including a berth in the Big 12 Tournament in 2006. Van Linder previously served as head coach at Southern Methodist University and Butler University, as an assistant coach at Butler, and as head coach at Linsley High School. Van Linder is a native of Galesburg, Michigan, and a graduate of Western Michigan University. (Photograph by Hardy Meredith.)

The cover photograph on the Ladyjack soccer media guide for 2008 featured the team's six seniors, including, from left to right, Lauren Fricks, Amanda Lackey, Amanda Alders, Jessica Cotton, Summer Bradfield, and Rachel Schwind. (Photograph by Hardy Meredith.)

Jessica Cotton was a first team All–Southland Conference selectee for 2007 and 2008, an All–Southland Conference tournament selectee, and a member of the First Team Academic All–Southland Conference team. Jessica started 19 of 20 games in 2007 as a defender. She had participated in soccer at Deer Park High School and for nine years in club leagues. (Photograph by Hardy Meredith.)

At right, Amanda Alders began her senior year as a Ladyjack as the team's all-time leader in career points and goals. She scored 74 career points and 32 goals through three seasons and was a Freshman of the Year selectee and a three-time All–Southland Conference selection. She twice earned a place on the Academic All–Southland Conference team. Below, Lauren Fricks was named Southland Conference Newcomer of the Year and to the all-conference tournament team in 2007. She is the only Ladyjack in school history to appear twice in the top 10 for assists in a single season. Lauren played soccer at Summit High School and led her team to a bi-district championship in 2003. (Both photographs by Hardy Meredith.)

Phil Olson became head coach of Stephen F. Austin State University's track and field program in 2000. His teams have won 11 cross-country and track and field championships and included 310 All Southland Conference selections, won 80 conference individual titles, set 157 school records, and had 26 NCAA qualifiers. His teams also included eight Academic All-Americans, and runner Rodney Joseph twice was named Southland Conference Student-Athlete of the Year. Previously Olson was an assistant coach at the University of Virginia and at Clemson University. Olson is shown conversing with thrower Colleen "Cookie" Lonergan. (Courtesy University News Service.)

Ashley Monteau is a two-time Southland Conference Female Cross Country Athlete of the Year, a six-time conference champion, and four-time NCAA All–South Central Region team member. Ashley was named conference Track Athlete of the Week twice. (Photograph by Hardy Meredith.)

Hammer thrower Frednisha Marshall from Tyler won the shot put at the 2009 Southland Conference outdoor championship with a mark of 48 feet, 7.5 inches. She set the school record in hammer throw three times. She earned All-America status for her third-place finish in the weight throw at the 2009 NCAA Indoor Championship. (Photograph by Hardy Meredith.)

Head Lumberjack basketball coach Danny Kaspar's first coaching job at Stephen F. Austin was as an assistant to coach Harry Miller from 1983 to 1986, and he also served on the staffs of coaching legends Billy Tubbs and Gene Iba. Kaspar, a graduate of the University of North Texas, coached at Incarnate Word University for nine seasons, winning 20 or more games each season. He succeeded Derek Allister at Stephen F. Austin State University in 2000, and through the 2008–2009 season, his teams won 158 games with only 102 losses for a percentage of .607. The Lumberjacks were Southland Conference cochampions in 2007–2008 and champions in 2008–2009, and Kaspar was named Coach of the Year in 2008. Here he instructs Josh Alexander before sending him into a game. (Photograph by Hardy Meredith.)

Shown at right are the Southland Conference trophy for men's basketball for the 2007–2008 season, won by the Stephen F. Austin State University Lumberjacks, and coach Danny Kasper's trophy as men's basketball conference Coach of the Year. (Photograph by Hardy Meredith.)

Members of the Lumberjack basketball team in 2008–2009 include, from left to right, (sitting) Cameron James, Preston Davis, Girod Adams, Jarrod McDaniel, Eric Bell, and Eddie Williams; (standing) Josh Alexander, Nick Shaw, Benson Akpan, Matt Kingsley, Aaron Smith, Jereal Scott, Walt Harris, and Zach Williams. This team won the Southland Conference in 2009, and Stephen F. Austin made its first-ever appearance in the NCAA tournament. (Photograph by Hardy Meredith.)

This cover for the 2008–2009 Lumberjack basketball media guide featured four of the team's five seniors. From left to right are Josh Alexander, Matt Kingsley, Eric Bell, and Nick Shaw. These seniors led the team to the Southland Conference championship. (Photograph by Hardy Meredith.)

Matt Kingsley takes a shot during a Southland Conference game played in the William R. Johnson Coliseum in 2007. Kingsley, a 6-foot, 9-inch center from Houston, was named to the second-team All–Southland Conference team in 2008 and won the conference's Player of the Year in 2009. He started all 32 games, finishing second in team scoring with 15.7 points per game and second in rebounds with 5.7 per game. (Photograph by Hardy Meredith.)

Head coach Brett Arrant squints in the sun as he watches Ladyjack tennis players in a match. Arrant has led the team for 15 years, averaging 10 wins per year. Below, members of the Ladyjack tennis squad pose for their media guide on the front drive of official residence of Pres. Baker and Janice Pattillo. From left to right are (first row) Gabriela Gadeva, Roxana Enica, Andreea Enica, Tatiana Smolnikova, Sanjana Kapur, and Christelle Kaempfer; (in the car) Mary Harrison; (standing behind the car) Jamie Williams and Nicole Schoenauer. (Both photographs by Hardy Meredith.)

Above left, former Lumberjack athletes O. A. "Bum" Phillips (left), who played football at Stephen F. Austin State University and later coached the Houston Oilers and New Orleans Saints in the National Football League; Van Samford (center), basketball standout and later dean of men at the university; and Travis Price (right), a former graduate of Stephen F. Austin State University who operated a business college in Nacogdoches, were honored during half-time ceremonies of a game played in the William R. Johnson Coliseum. Below left, Bob Sitton, retired director of the Stephen F. Austin Alumni Association, greets Terry Black, a former Ladyjack basketball player coached by program founder Sue Gunter who had returned to campus for activities honoring the Ladyjacks' legendary coach, including the naming of the suite occupied by women's basketball coaches in the William R. Johnson Coliseum for Gunter. (Both photographs by Hardy Meredith.)

Lee Ann Riley took over as head coach of the Ladyjack basketball team prior to the 2001–2002 season and took home both the regular season and tournament championships that year, winning 24 games and losing only 6. Riley played at Tyler Junior College and Baylor University before beginning her coaching career as a graduate assistant at Tyler Junior College. She also served as assistant coach at New Mexico State University and at Stephen F. Austin State University before returning to Tyler Junior College as head coach. Riley worked as associate head coach at the University of Missouri for one season before joining the Ladyjacks as head coach. Her record at Stephen F. Austin State University through the 2008–2009 season is 131 wins and 105 losses, with a .555 winning percentage, and she was named Southland Conference Coach of the Year in 2006. Her teams have made two NCAA tournament appearances. (Photograph by Hardy Meredith.)

LaToya Mills (left), who played on teams coached by Lee Ann Riley, is the only Ladyjack in the program's history who was selected for the All–Southland Conference team all four years of eligibility. Below is Charity Egenti, the Southland Conference Player of the Year for 2006–2007. The Ladyjacks enjoyed 21 victories, with 11 wins in conference play, and only had 12 losses, 5 of those against Southland Conference opponents. They were invited to play in the Women's National Invitation Tournament. (Both photographs by Hardy Meredith.)

Nell Fortner came to Stephen F. Austin as an assistant women's basketball coach when Gary Blair coached the Ladyjacks. She later served as assistant coach for the 1996 Olympic U.S. National Team, which won the gold medal in the Olympic Games, and as head coach of the U.S. National Team from 1997 to 2000. Her U.S. National teams won 101 games, more than any other coach. Fortner later served as head coach of the Indiana Fever in the Women's National Basketball Association and at Auburn University; she brought that team to SFA to play the Ladyjacks. Fortner, left, instructs an unidentified player in a game played in the William R. Johnson Coliseum. (Photograph by Hardy Meredith.)

Coach Debbie Humphreys began working with the Ladyjack volleyball team in 1988, and to date, her teams have won seven Southland Conference championships and made NCAA tournament appearances in 1994, 1997, 1999, and 2006. Her teams established a 62-game winning streak in conference play from 2004 to the 2007 season. Humphreys has been named Southland Conference Coach of the Year four times, and her teams have included 57 all-conference selections. Her teams have won more games than any other coach's in conference history. A native of Rochester, Illinois, Humphreys played volleyball for three years at Texas Tech University and was named the team's most valuable player in her senior year; she was also a finalist for Academic All-America. (Photograph by Hardy Meredith.)

Standout players of coach Debbie Humphries's 2008 team included, at right, M. C. Bottles, No. 1, who became a first team All–Southland Conference designee, and No. 12, Lauren Railey, who was named Southland Conference Freshman of the Year in 2005 and was named to the All–Southland Conference second team in 2006 and to the All–Southland Conference first team in 2007 and 2008. Ladyjack freshman Melissa Miksch, No. 15, is in the center. Below is No. 6, Sydney Milburn, who played in 15 matches in 2008 and had 89 digs, and No. 3, Laurel Kuepker, a 2008 All–Southland Conference Honorable Mention and Southland Conference Defensive Player of the Week four times during the 2008 season. Other players are, from left to right, Paloma Buckner, Amber Williams-Roberts, Melissa Miksch, and Ashley Bailey. (Both photographs by Hardy Meredith.)

Ladyjack softball coach Gay McNutt (left) joined the athletic staff at Stephen F. Austin State University in time for the 2008 season after serving as a head coach for 13 years—at Northwestern State University (seven years) and Southern Mississippi University (six years)—where her teams won 372 games and five conference titles. In her first year as Stephen F. Austin's head coach, McNutt's team won their first Southland Conference tournament title and made the school's first NCAA tournament appearance. Below is the Ladyjacks softball team for 2008–2009. From left to right are (first row) Benet Higgs, Monica Hirsch, Karissa Jones, Canndise Juarez, Kim Daley, and Kari Hugie; (second row) student trainer Katie Jordan, Jessica Arana, Moriah Davis, Crystal Garcia, Michelle Huffman, Malina Meng, Briana Bishop, Krista Hallmark, and Jana Joyner; (third row) manager Alex Meng, assistant manager Craig Snider, Lauren Luetge, Debra Boles, Kayla Gutowski, Sabrina Johnston, Monika Covington, Kendal Harper, Amber Price, Ashley Struchtemeyer, and coach Gay McNutt. (Both photographs by Hardy Meredith.)

Head football coach J. C. Harper took over the program at Stephen F. Austin State University in 2007, when coach Robert McFarland accepted an assistant coaching position at Iowa State University. Previously, Harper had served on McFarland's staff as defensive coordinator. He played for four years as a Clemson University Tiger and began his coaching career as a graduate assistant under Mack Brown at the University of North Carolina, then as a graduate assistant coach at Notre Dame University with Lou Holtz. Harper also served as defensive coordinator at Southwest Missouri State University, Northwestern State University, McNeese State University, and Western Michigan University before coming to Stephen F. Austin State University. (Photograph by Hardy Meredith.)

Injuries plagued coach J. C. Harper's football team in 2007, but the Lumberjacks played hard in every game. Getting ready for a play, above, are Lloyd Ligons (No. 9), Tobi Kaiyewu (No. 66), Bradley Chmelar (No. 79), Joe Savoie (no. 88), Jesse Funk (No. 77), and Blake Hinton (No. 68). The player on the far right appears to be Josh Steger (No. 70), and the helmet to the right of No. 66 appears to be either Danny Southall or Jeremy Moses, both quarterbacks. Below, the Lumberjacks enter Homer Bryce Stadium through a purple haze to begin a game, with linebacker Tim Knicky displaying his skull-and-crossbones signature. (Both photographs by Hardy Meredith.)

The rivalry between Lumberjack and Ladyjack athletic programs and Bearcat teams representing Sam Houston State University in Huntsville is the oldest and most intense in the Southland Conference. Perhaps an indication of that rivalry is the development of a trophy displaying two pistols, which is exchanged on the basis of victory in the annual football game called the Battle of the Pineywoods. The plaque for the Battle of the Pineywoods is formidable but not as large as Chief Caddo, which is awarded annually to the victor in the game against the Northwestern State Demons. The chief, who stands 7 feet, 6 inches tall and weighs more than 300 pounds, was carved from a 2,000-pound black gum log in 1961. When Chief Caddo is in residence in the Champions Room of Stephen F. Austin State University's athletic department headquarters, the ceiling is modified to accommodate his high headdress. (Both photographs by Hardy Meredith.)

Athletic director Robert Hill and assistant director John Branch stand near the entrance to their offices in the field house, located in Homer Bryce Stadium. Hill, on the left, joined the athletic staff in 1987 as director of sports information. He became assistant athletic director for business affairs in 1990, associate director for internal affairs in 1998, and athletic director in 2004. Eleven teams have won championships in the Southland Conference during Hill's tenure as director. Branch, on the right, has worked in the athletic department for over a decade and as assistant director for internal affairs since 2005. Branch oversees fund-raising, external development, and marketing for the Department of Athletics. Prior to joining the athletic staff, Branch worked as an intern with the Dallas Cowboys. (Photograph by Hardy Meredith.)

At right, Greg "Buck" Payne, equipment manager, puts away shoulder pads in the equipment room, a duty he has performed at Stephen F. Austin State University for three decades. Payne is a member of the Athletic Equipment Managers Association and twice the recipient of the Knight-Packard Equipment Award. Buck served as an equipment manager for the Houston Oilers until 1979. Below, assistant athletic trainer Loree McCary has held the primary responsibility for the care and rehabilitation of Ladyjack athletes for two decades. She is a member of the National Athletic Trainers' Association and is the senior woman's administrator for the athletic department. McCary is a graduate of Kansas State University and of the graduate program at the University of Florida. (Both photographs by Hardy Meredith.)

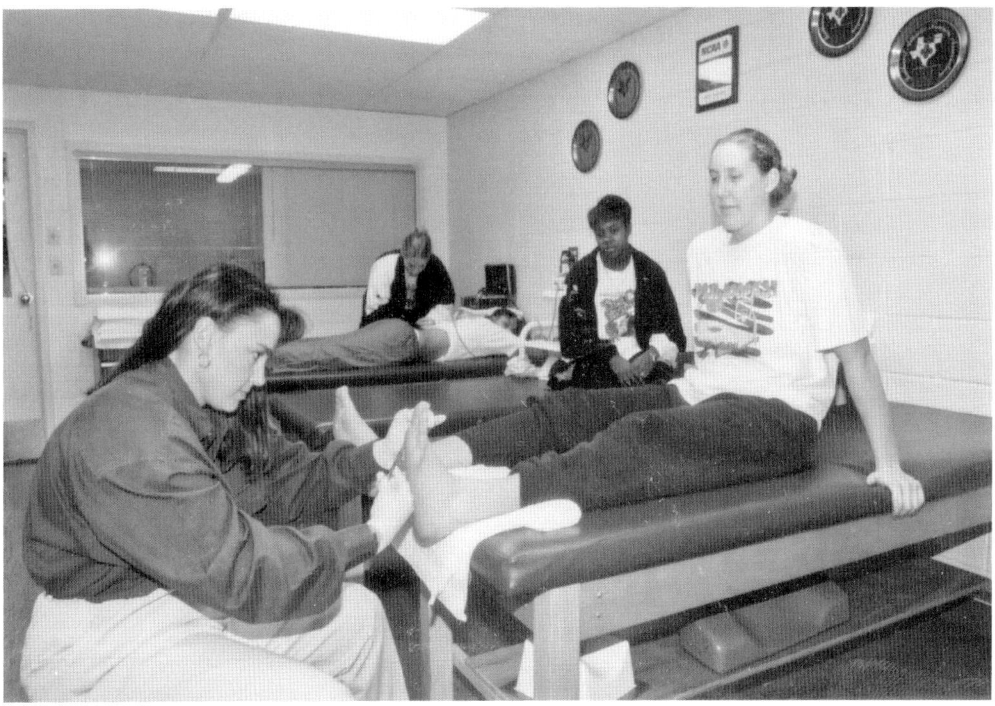

Steve Westbrook is vice president for university affairs at Stephen F. Austin State University. Westbrook began his career in 1981 as program advisor for the University Center and then advanced to coordinator of programs, director of student activities, and director of student affairs. He is a member of the American College Personnel Association and state and national personnel associations and served as chair of the National Association for Campus Activities. Westbrook holds undergraduate and graduate degrees from Stephen F. Austin State University and is married to the former Dayna Reed, an outstanding Ladyjack basketball player and coach of women's basketball at Douglass High School. (Photograph by Hardy Meredith.)

Pres. Baker Pattillo, left, and former athletic director Steve McCarty are in a familiar setting: witnessing a contest involving student athletes from Stephen F. Austin State University. President Pattillo, who holds two degrees from Stephen F. Austin State University, joined the university's staff in 1966 when he was named assistant director of placement and financial aid. He became director of that division in 1970 and dean of student services two years later. Pattillo became vice president for student affairs in 1979 and president of the university in 2006. McCarty served as assistant director and then director of athletics. Gov. Rick Perry appointed McCarty to the university's board of regents in 2009. (Photograph by Hardy Meredith.)

In 2009, the staff of the Department of Athletics (above) included, from left to right, (first row) Joyce Campbell, Marsha Montes, Darba Rollins, and Joan Taylor; (second row) Cheryl Mott, Sandy Miller, Lauren Adams, Amber Burdge, Kathy Springfield, Loree McCary, and Christal Shaw; (third row) Greg Payne, director Robert Hill, Matt Fenley, Trey Younger, John Branch, Ben Rikard, James Dixon, Jeremy Stolfa, Rob Meyers, and Brian Ross. Below are members of the 2008–2009 cross-country team. From left to right are (first row) Bette Fleming-Wood, Stephanie Ganter, Randi Wymer, Megan Jenkins, Marie Flores, Brittany Robertson, Amy Shackleford, Meredith Blocker, and Heather Adams; (second row) Assistant coach Cody Clark, Xavier Rodriguez, Harmon McClanahan, Mitch Ownbey, Elliot Starcevich, Sam Hulse, Keith Mahipala, Dennis Yeats, James Lopez, and head cross-country coach Lou Snelling. (Both photographs by Hardy Meredith.)

Cheerleaders for Ladyjack and Lumberjack athletic teams in 2008–2009 are pictured on the track in Homer Bryce Stadium. From left to right are (first row) Shelly Eagan, Ashley Tucker, Courtney Patrick, Chelsea Craiker, and Samantha Frazer; (second row) Jeremy Gunter, Cody Kirkland, David Bowden, Michael Seitzer, Adam Mickelson, Steve Johnson, Tim Wegner, Alec Heffron, Jason Larkins, James Brown, Jason Williams, Brent Heironimus, coach Trisha O'Connor, Jerrod Vanover, Dustin Moore, assistant coach Scott Holland, and advisor Michael Preston. Cheerleaders not shown are Chris Kurkjian, Laura Medved, Cameron Odom, mascot Steven Staines, Cassie Valentine, Casey Harris, and Yvette Quinones. At right, kicker Cory Long is pictured shortly after his field goal led the Lumberjacks to a 48-45 victory over Southeast Louisiana State University. (Both photographs by Hardy Meredith.)

Associate athletic director Matt Fenley, left, serves as Stephen F. Austin State University's compliance officer for NCAA and Southland Conference relations and is in charge of student services. Fenley joined the university's athletic staff in 1990 after serving as assistant athletic director at Sam Houston State University for three years. Fenley coached at Pittsburg State University in Kansas and also at Benedictine College, where he had also played football. In addition to his administrative duties, Fenley also joins Rob Meyers, athletics assistant director for business affairs, to broadcast Lumberjack football games at home and on the road. With Fenley is Lauren Adams, a former athlete and now a graduate student and administrative assistant in the Department of Athletics. (Photograph by Hardy Meredith.)

Members of Stephen F. Austin's board of regents gathered for the opening of the university's new tennis complex, located on Wilson Drive, in September 2008. Pres. Baker Pattillo and Jerry and Candace Schlief cut the ribbon to open the complex. Jerry Schlief is a graduate of the university, and he and Candace provided funding for the tennis center. Pictured are, from left to right, (kneeling) Andreea Enica, Roxana Enica, Mary Harrison, Christelle Kaempfer, Tatiana Smolnikova, and Jamie Williams; (standing) Sanjana Kapur, Nicole Schoenauer, regent Paul Pond, student regent Stephanie Tracy, regents Melvin White, Valerie Ertz, and Richard Boyer, President Pattillo, athletic director Robert Hill, Jerry and Candice Schlief, tennis coach Brett Arrant, regents Bob Garrett and Carlos Amaral, regents chairman Joe Max Green, regent James Dickerson, and Gabriela Gadeva, with the ribbon. (Photograph by Hardy Meredith.)

Head coach J. C. Harper, left, took over the Lumberjack program in the fall of 2006 when his predecessor, Robert McFarland, accepted an assistant coaching position at Iowa State University. Harper had been defensive coordinator for McFarland, but he faced a rebuilding year. Harper's team fared better in the 2008 season, when it won four games. Below, the Lumberjack bench joins players on the field in celebration. From left to right are Lumberjacks Aaron Ray, Brandon Scott, Dominique Edison, and Roderick Warren, and coaches Aaron De La Torre, Harper, and Chris Truax. (Both photographs by Hardy Meredith.)

Rob Meyers, the "Voice of the Lumberjacks" who provides play-by-play radio coverage of all Lumberjack football and basketball games, is also an assistant athletic director in charge of business affairs. Meyers joined the university's athletic staff as sports information officer in 1996 and advanced to assistant director in 2004. Meyers spent 10 years as director of news and sports at several radio stations, including two in the Nacogdoches area, and three years in the newspaper business. (Photograph by Hardy Meredith.)

Paige Pattillo, the daughter of Dr. Baker and Dr. Janice Pattillo, served as a featured twirler with the Nacogdoches High School Band, four years as a featured twirler with the Lumberjack Band while attending Stephen F. Austin State University, and two years as a featured twirler with the Longhorn Band while attending law school at the University of Texas in Austin. Paige returned to Nacogdoches following the completion of her legal education and works in the office of the county attorney for Nacogdoches County. (Photograph by Hardy Meredith.)

Coach Danny Kaspar cut the basket from the hoop following his Lumberjacks' victory over the University of Texas—San Antonio Road Runners to win the 2009 Southland Conference Basketball Tournament championship in Katy. This earned Stephen F. Austin the conference's automatic bid to the NCAA tournament. (Photograph courtesy Hardy Meredith.)

Eric Bell, 5-foot, 3-inch guard on the Lumberjack basketball team, was the smallest player in the nation in NCAA competition during the 2008–2009 season. Despite his size, Bell was named Newcomer of the Year and was an Honorable Mention on the All–Southland Conference team in 2007–2008, when he started all 32 games and led the conference in assists (5.7 per game) and assist-to-turnover (2.5). Bell played at DeSoto High School and McLennan County Community College before moving to the Lumberjacks. Guarding Bell is Brian Marks, a 7-foot, 2-inch player for Central Arkansas University. (Photograph by Hardy Meredith.)

The Lumberjacks played the Orangemen of Syracuse University in the NCAA tournament's first round in Miami, Florida. Lumberjacks (in purple uniforms) are, from left to right, Nick Shaw, Josh Alexander, Girod Adams, and Eddie Williams. (Photograph courtesy Hardy Meredith.)

The Lumberjack baseball team opened its home season on March 7, 2009, in Jaycee Field (above), a remodeled stadium located in the Pete Smith Baseball Complex operated by the City of Nacogdoches adjacent to Loop 224 and Old Tyler Road. The stadium seats 750 fans, with a covered central portion that has backed seats instead of benches. Coach Johnny Cardenas's team began its fourth year of competition in the Southland Conference, and Chris Connally and Chad Massengale assisted Cardenas with coaching duties. At right, old-timers Chuck Rawlinson, left, and Mark Moseley, two legendary kickers on the Lumberjack football team, came back to Homer Bryce Stadium for hall of fame inductions. Moseley played at Stephen F. Austin State University from 1966 to 1968 before beginning a professional career with the Washington Redskins and other teams in the National Football League. Rawlinson, who played from 1988 to 1991, holds Lumberjack records for most extra points in an individual game and in a season, most extra point attempts, most extra points, most field goal attempts, most field goals, and longest kick. (Both photographs by Hardy Meredith.)

Gary Blair brought his Texas A&M Aggie women's basketball team to Nacogdoches to play an early-season game against the Ladyjacks in the fall of 2008. When Blair coached the Ladyjacks from 1985 through 1993, he found it difficult to arrange for top 10 teams to come to Nacogdoches. On December 2, 2008, he brought his Aggies team, then ranked No. 4 in the nation, to the site of his former assignment at Stephen F. Austin State University. While here, Blair was inducted into the Ladyjack Hall of Fame. Holding the plaque certifying his induction, Blair, center, poses with Pres. Baker Pattillo, left, and athletic director Robert Hill, right, in William R. Johnson Coliseum. Below, Trisha O'Connor, coordinator of the Stephen F. Austin spirit program and head coach of the university's cheerleaders, wears six Division One championship rings she has won—three as a cheerleader and three as a coach. O'Connor graduated from Stephen F. Austin State University in 2005. (Both photographs by Hardy Meredith.)

Hardy Meredith has been a fixture at Stephen F. Austin State University since the fall of 1996. As the university's official photographer, he attends all major events on the campus or wherever officials or students represent the university. Hardy is a familiar figure patrolling the sidelines at games and matches in which Lumberjacks and Ladyjacks participate, a camera in hand and another strapped around his neck snapping pictures and storing up memories. (Photograph by Cody Derouen.)